C000070421

# Bombay to Birmingham

## Satish D H Thaker

Bombay to Birmingham


Copyright © 2012 Satish D H Thaker

ISBN: **9798645814403**

# Disclaimer

ISBN **9798645814403**

*Effort has been made to ensure that the information in this book is accurate and complete; however, the author and the publisher do not warrant the accuracy of the information, text, and graphics contained within the book due to the rapidly changing nature of science, research, known and unknown facts, and information available on the internet.*

*The author and the publisher do not accept any responsibility for errors, omission, or contrary interpretation of the subject matter herein. It assumes no patent liability regarding the use of the information contained. This book is presented solely for motivational and informational purposes.*

*This book, as well as all names, places, events etc. are a work of non-fiction. Any resemblance or likeness to any person, living or dead, place, or organisation is purely coincidental.*

# A SPECIAL NOTE OF THANKS

54 years ago, in 1966, dad sent me to UK, against all the odds. My uncles were against the idea. I failed the 1st year at Bhavan's College, even still, he planned my journey to London. He kept the plan close to his heart, until the time was right. My mum heavy heartedly said yes, and reluctantly supported dad, so that I could have a better future.

Thank you to all my uncles and aunties, cousins and nieces who helped to dig out the history and the stories about Aden in the 50s & 60s, so I could record it in the book. Also, thanks for the stories about the struggles and the settlement, about the friendships and achievements; as well as the stories about the tradition and the transition.

To my wife, Kirtida, son Devdutt, daughter-in-law Krishna, daughter Puja (Jaid), who all encouraged me and showed enthusiasm in my writing. My wife has the patience of a mountain. She sacrificed her time and put up with me while I spent hours writing. I had unwritten accountability to the Thaker family.

I'm grateful to Shantibhai and Taruben Patira, Babubhai and Manubhai Vakharia, Kadarbhai and Sugraben, and Kishore Shrimankar families for supporting me prior to leaving Aden, and after.

Kantibhai (Shankarbhai) and Kantaben Khimji (London), Chimanlal and Dahiben Desai (Birmingham), Gurudayal singh Semi family (Birmingham) and Ramesh Lalbhai Patel (Leicester) for clearing the runway by integrating me in their family. Without their support, I would have struggled to settle and survive.

Satish D H Thaker

# CONTENTS

# Bombay to Birmingham
### By:  Satish D H Thaker

### Introduction

## My Journey

## What I intended and what materialised.

### Initial plan

### Bombay to Aden by steamer

*Plan changed in Aden*

Aden to Cairo by Aeroplane

Cairo to Athens by Aeroplane

Athens to Munich by Aeroplane

Munich to Stuttgart by train

Instead of travelling back to Munich and then fly to London.

*Plan changed in Stuttgart*

Stuttgart to Frankfort by train

Frankfort to London by Aeroplane.  And settle in London

*Plan change in London.*

London to Birmingham by train to Snowhill Station.

# <u>18<sup>th</sup> April 1966</u>

I was stepping into a new life, the first chapter of an unknown future.

There is a famous saying, you don't know what you don't know, what you don't know.'

Fear, anxiety, excitement, and sadness all rushed through me in a torrent of emotions. There was no certainty about when I would be coming back to visit my mum, Manorama, my uncle, Navalchandra, my aunty, Pushpaben, or my nana and nanny (my mother's parents). Nana had always been an energetic entrepreneur, he invented the hand-held sharpeners for shaving blades, and opened the first match-stick factory in Ludhiana (now in Pakistan) before the separation. My nanny was full of wisdom and always smiling. I would miss them all terribly.

I was scared because for five days, I was going to be a stranger amongst strangers, a lonely soul on a steamer. On the other hand, I was excited because I was about to become independent, I would have no accountability to anyone for the next five days.

# Time line

Depart Bombay 18 April 1966

Arrived in Aden 23 April 1966
Depart Aden 16 July 1966 to Cairo
Depart Cairo 22 July 1966 to Athens
Depart Athens 27 July 1966 to Munich
Depart Frankfort 4 Aug 1966 to London
Depart London 5 Aug 1966 to Birmingham

# 1 LIFE ON A STEAMER

A deafening horn blasted through the air. The metal surface juddered violently, for a moment it felt like it was all going to slide away from under us. We stumbled, pushing against each other. Just in time I caught the trembling hand of a grey-haired lady before she crashed against the row of rusty railings. She looked at me with genuine appreciation in her eyes.

'Thank you,' she muttered before the curses of the crowd drowned out any further speech. People were gripping to the metal railings, their knuckles going white, and their eyes wide as their blood pressure soared. Everyone was wondering the same thing – what was that?

A final blast sounded and there were goodbyes all-round. To the west the sky blazed orange as the sun sank down towards the horizon. The steamer started to shake as it prepared to move away from the crowded docks.

There was a sudden commotion worse than being in the fish market. The disturbance was on the starboard side near where I was standing, on the dock and the gangway-the bridge.

'Teree Maaki, sala dekh-ke chal naa,' the red-shirted coolie shouted to the black-shirted coolie. He rushed up the gangway, struggling to come up as he was balancing two metal trunks on his head with one hand, and a mattress rolled up in his other sweaty arm pit.

'Mataji chalooo - jaldi chalooo,' he kept on rushing the lady behind him, trying to push through the busy, unstable gangway. It wobbled beneath them as he tried to barge through. A young lady wearing a tatty light blue sari, having a tug of war with a young girl, was struggling to keep up with the coolie. The man following a few steps behind her, wearing white cotton salwar, and a kameez, was presumably her husband.

Over the top he wore an eccentric dusty black jacket along with a white cotton sweaty Gandhi tophi-a side cap. He had a cotton bag in his left hand full of vegetables. With the other hand he pulled along an unhappy, screaming, revolting young boy. Sweat dripped from his forehead on to his eyelids before it slid down on to his cheeks. His face and ears were dark red and his eyes wide open, a sign of high blood pressure. It was impossible for anyone not to notice that he looked like a fish out of water. Assumedly the family had been harassed at customs and immigration.

There were frantic movements all around as the black-shirt coolies shouted orders in their local "Kokni" slang, preparing to pull away the rusty gangway from the steamer. The red-shirt coolies were in a hurry to cash-up with the arguing passengers and get down to the docks before the gangway was removed.

The people crowded on the dock and the passengers crammed onto the steamer could hardly see each other, yet they waved frantically and shouted at the top of their voices, giving last-minute instructions and farewells. Some had tears rolling down their cheeks.

The black-shirt coolies finally pulled away the rusty iron stepping bridge with a hideous screeching noise.

It was 18th April 1966, the experience of a lifetime. I was only 18 yrs. and 22 days old. The hustle and bustle of the docks slowly slipped away into the distance. A frothy trail followed in our wake, as the docks faded away into the horizon. The steamer sliced through the dirty, murky brown water - the colour a result of the Bombay gutter system, and cut us a path towards the dark blue of the Arabian Ocean.

I was on Muzzafir, one of the Mogul-line steamers. It was the days when most of us travelled in economy class on the lower deck. The upper classes, the rich travellers, preferred P&Os' fully air-conditioned modern steamers.

There was a chill in the air. On my first evening on the deserted deck I was feeling depressed and isolated. Other passengers were busy securing their belongings to the metal bunk beds on the lower deck. I drifted away, daydreaming. My thoughts were at war as I kept on asking myself, was this the right decision?

Yes! Shouted one half while the other begrudgingly admitted that there was no turning back now. I would have to take whatever came my way next, whether I liked it or not. It was my decision, and it was a stubborn one at that.

It was my first experience of travelling alone on a long journey, at such a young age, I felt like a pioneer among the Thakers.
Many questions clouded my brain.

Why? Why was I leaving Bombay? Why?

I kept on asking myself, over and over again.

I felt like a failure. I had failed the first year of Science at the Bhavan's College, Andheri (W), Bombay. Before that, I had never failed so badly during my school days.

I was *the student*, the one that others looked up to as an "Adarsh" student. The best. I was the head prefect, the Captain of the ACC, even the (acting) principle of the school! Well maybe that one was only for a week when the senior students took on the role of schoolteachers. I was the best. Yet, now I felt like a total failure. I had nothing to show for my work in those days. The last thing I wanted to think about was my studies or the books. I wanted to be in Aden with my dad to help with business. Perhaps I would learn a trick or two.
Was it a rash decision?

Was I too sceptical and judgemental?

I felt worthless and ashamed. I was a stranger amongst strangers, travelling on my own.

Indian families traditionally carried their own rations for long journeys, they were mainly vegetarians and so all their meals consisted of vegetables. Theplas (spicy chapattis) and pickle were typically on the menu, along with loose teas, as the use of tea bags hadn't spread to India yet, sugar and tea-masala for the traditional Gujarati tea. Without sweets, Gujarati food is incomplete. Ladoos, the sweet balls were the most popular and convenient choice as they would last for a long journey. Families would also carry paraffin stoves, pots, and pans to cook their food at their own convenience.

What is diabetic? The word "diabetic" hadn't surfaced in the 60s so no one worried about the amount of sweets they ate.

The on-board kitchen staff were Muslim. The vegetarian passengers didn't approve of the kitchen food as it was cooked by the meat-eating Muslims and there were no requirements for the use of separate cooking utensils.

I was the black sheep of the clan, a meat-eater. The Khema, a minced lamb curry, was my favourite.

The Gujarati families offered me home cooked food, more often they insisted upon it as I was travelling on my own. While it was a kindness, I wanted to be independent, not pitied all the time. It felt over-bearing and forceful, despite the good intent. So, at mealtimes I would disappear to the other deck, avoiding the mothering ladies.

I ended up making friends with the junior crew officers. We would play table tennis together and talk. Any uniforms were fascinating for me. I was inquisitive and wanted to explore the ship. The thundering pounding noise that came from the metal walls all around was the first curiosity to be investigated. I wanted to discover the source of the noise.

However, the mutton curry aroma and the mouth-watering scent of freshly baked chapatti drew me towards the kitchen instead. The innocent smile and the hungry expression on my face revealed everything. The elderly cook gestured for me to take a seat. We conversed in Hindi and Urdu. It was great to make a new friend.

I was offered a Thali (a flat round metal plate with raised sides) with a large, but not round, chapatti. It was a typical Muslim chapatti, not as good as my mum's Gujarati chapatti! Along with the chapatti was a bowl full of mutton curry with a layer of dark red oily gravy.
I polished off the meal leaving the plate clean. That pleased the head cook. He was happy for me to visit the kitchen whenever I felt like it.

Night was drawing in. It was time to explore the steamer. The engine room was deep down in the hull. As I drew closer, the thundering, pounding noise was getting louder. Descending into the bowels of the ship the air became warmer and the smell of hot oil was strong in the air. As there was no sign telling me "No entry", I entered the engine room.

Inquisitiveness took precedence over fear.

From the bottom of the stairs, the small-looking engine mechanic in his dark-stained boiler suit, looked up at me. His face and hands were covered in grease, and he wasn't wearing ear defenders. As I was wearing leather shoes with metal studs, I was hesitant at descending the slippery metal stairs. I gripped the warm, shaky side rails as firmly as I could. The engineer gave me a nod and eye gesture to indicate I should stay where I was and watch from a safe distance. Conversation was unfortunately impossible due to the noise, so the facial expression and hand signals were the only options.

From my position at the top of the stairs I watched the eight giant pounding pistons, each set a few degrees behind each other, following, and trying to catch-up in perfect rhythm. Mesmerised by the tempo, size and steaming of the engine turbines, I kept on staring, admiring the engineering ingenuity.

I must have stayed long enough to get a headache because by the time I returned to the top deck, the noise of the pistons was still roaring in my ears. It reassured me though that we were on the move. The deadly cold sea was still far beyond the horizon, but we were on our way.

The upper deck was still deserted. I stood holding onto the cold metal railings. In the distance I caught glimpses of flickering lights as other ships passed by. The night was dim, but not dark. The twinkling stars above were hope for many. A gentle breeze softly kissed my cheeks. When I looked back to the water, I noticed large fish surfacing and following us, hoping for scraps of food.

Suddenly, a shiver ran down my spine as I realised that it would be a 100-foot drop to the water from the top deck. I stepped back from the cold, sticky railings.

'Help! Someone overboard! A body in the water!' no one would hear if even, I screamed at the top of my voice. Who would sound an alarm? Who would alert someone or get help? There was no one else besides me on the deck. The roaring sound of the engine would dampen the sounds of splashing and screams for help. There would be no chance of rescue.

I suppressed a shudder. I didn't want to chance meeting those fish in the freezing black water. Instead, I backed away from the edge and sat on the cold damp bench, it froze me to the bones with horrible thoughts chasing around my mind.

For a while I drifted away in cigar-smoked memories.
The 50 plus bunk beds were on the lower deck, situated in a large open space. The dim lights inside gave the place a gloomy atmosphere. Two people shared each bunk bed. I was young enough to use the upper bunk bed. Little children and babies shared a bed with their mums. Able adults and youngsters slept on the top of the bunk bed, while the elderly slept on the lower bed. Most families were travelling together.

On the third night at sea, the steamer rocked from side to side. Both sides of the railings kept coming too damn close to the water, the ship's side seam disappearing in the water. Huge waves splashed onto the upper deck.

I have no shame in admitting that the rough sea was not to my liking!

I wasn't a sailor. I was seasick. Most of the other travelers were too. With full stomachs after eating, tucked away in bed, trying to cling to the metal bed sides, the lower bunk was the wrong place to be. We realised our stomachs wouldn't be staying full for long.

Walking was challenging. The turmoil of the steamer on a rough sea was an unpleasant experience for most of us. We couldn't hold food down for long. As the sea became rougher, we started throwing up, downwards and outwards, sprinkling vile stinky spew all over. It sprayed everything in its path, be it hands, face or bed sheets. Lumps of gooey food spread over everything. There was no escape from the overpowering smell of vomit. We stayed in bed to avoid the slippery floor. Only a handful of experienced regular travelers climbed out to help others.

The next day, the sun appeared, tearing the clouds apart with its rays. What a blessing. The sea's waves settled into light ripples.

The crew armed with water hoses, washed the messy deck floor with sea water. The fresh air brought life back on the deck.

The women started pumping the paraffin stoves to light-up and prepare tea and breakfast. After the night's experience, our empty stomachs were rumbling, ready for the next meal.

# 2 SCHOOL DAYS IN INDIA

In 1958, my younger cousin Vasant (Haku) and I, were day students at the Hansraj Morarji High school in Andheri (the Bombay suburb). My elder brother, Jitubhai, and Vasant's elder brother,

Vinod, attended the boys' boarding school. They had the privilege of learning horse riding, playing cricket or football, and jumping in the swimming pool. For us, the younger ones, we amused ourselves in the evenings and weekends in the flower garden, climbing fruit trees.

Our parents were brave enough to be in Aden in the 1960s, while the independent struggle was on the rise.

We were a bit of a handful for mum's parents, Nana and Nanny, Uncle, and Aunty, our guardians. The set-up was that the older children went to boarding school while the younger ones went to the day-school, but it didn't work out.

They shifted us at the end of the academy year to Sanjeevan Vidhyalay, the boys' boarding school in Panchgini, Mahabaleshvar, in Maharashtra state.

They divided the boarding school into three houses, Red, Green and Blue. They singled me out by putting me in the Red House while my elder brother and cousins stayed together in the Blue House. Most students were local Maharastrians, a few from Bombay, NRIs (non-resident Indians from Uganda and Kenya) and a few from the Gujarat. The school had armed guards protecting it from the tigers which ventured out during the night from the surrounding jungle.

In Panchgini, there were a few dedicated boarding schools for the girls, the Catholics, the Parsees, and for the privileged children from the higher societies, such as politicians, Bollywood actors, business tycoons etc.

The Mahabaleshvar is a hill station rich with eucalyptus and fruit trees and buzzing with vivid exotic birds. Families from the big cities come to the hill station for the summer vacation, getting away from the crazy crowds.

Old Bollywood movie clips are full of songs with the background sceneries featuring romantic beauty spots of the Mahabaleshvar'

Mahabaleshvar landmark is the Panchgini (Panch=five, gini=mountains), a fusion of five mountains. The tips of the five mountains are joint and flat, a Natural phenomenon.

During sports sessions, we would run up to the top and play football and hockey on three full size pitches. We used all three pitches during the sport sessions. There was no road to drive up, only a narrow path for walking, jogging, or running. A handful of spectators would take up the challenge to get the top to watch us. The air gets thinner and fresher as you climb up to the top.

Playing cricket one evening, they positioned me on Short, just behind the Silly-mid-on. The bowler started his run; I followed the baller, and then the ball as it left the spin, my head turned to the batsman, a good shot.

A splendid shot in fact – heading right for me. Before I could duck, it slammed straight into my face.

It broke my specs and lens, but luckily my eyeballs were still intact. That was it. I hated playing cricket! No more cricket for me. Since then, I felt uneasy every time I was on the pitch; I gave excuse after excuse to avoid playing.

Sorry cricket lovers hate me or love me, but it's not my game.

On my return visit in 2016, after five decades, I didn't appreciate many of the changes which had occurred. Where there had only been a handful of cars on the hill station previously, it had been replaced with traffic jams and limited parking spaces. Where the boarding schools had once dominated, the jam and juices factories had sprung up. They had built a tarmac road up to the base of the hill, just 10 m short from the top. The horse-riding business was flourishing on the sports pitch, with overgrown grass and potholes. There were even young couples scattered around taking selfies, looking for a romantic beauty spot to capture.

Shame!

I was so disappointed and sad.

As change is inevitable, there's no choice but to accept it.

# 3 GURUKUL SUPA

Another year and another move in 1960, for all of us. My two cousins moved to the Rajkumar College, to Rajkot in Gujarat State. Most of the Thakers were in Rajkot. My elder brother Jitendra, two younger siblings Arvind (Sanu), Rajiv (Raju), and I moved to another boarding school, Gurukul Vidhyamandir Supa.

To the locals knew it as "Supa-Gurukul". It wasn't far from the Navsari, the city where in the 8th century the Parsees, Persians who descended from Persian Zoroastrians, immigrated to India to avoid religious persecution by the Muslims.

The Supa-Gurukul teachings based on Aryasamaj beliefs and values: comradeship, self-resilience, adaptability, respect for elders and gurus, love towards children and animals, sharing, and helping the needy.

I stayed there for five years until I completed my graduation. Supa-Gurukul was the first milestone of my character building. Other schools and large establishments biased towards the Western way of thinking but lacking in good values.

The boarding school was on the bank of the river Purna, five acres of fertile land full of mango trees of different varieties. There was also a large farming plot for the teaching of farming and animal husbandry as part of the curriculum. That was as well as the full-size football pitch.

There were three main large brick buildings.

> The living accommodation was a single-storey square building, with an open courtyard in the centre
> A two-storey building for academic studies
> Another single-storey square building was dedicated to the kitchen and dining area

The main entrance to the dormitories was an archway opening in the center of the south side of the square building. On the top of the archway was only one room, designated to the head of the boarding school. The four teacher caretakers, "Asrama-Dhyax", strategically placed in the four corners of the building. Each teacher could monitor the right- and left-hand-side flanks. Each side had students from separate years. The rooms had two rows of 15 metal beds, with a walkway in between. The bed was for seating and studying and sleeping. The metal trunk under the bed was the only storage for our belongings. No photos, no wrist-watch, and no cameras allowed. They permitted us to have very few personal possessions. It was a lesson on how to survive off the bare minimum.

I started in the 7th standard, on the right-hand side of the primary entrance. The teacher in-charge was a skilful hockey player, but he had some health issues. Every time it hit him with a hockey ball to a bare shin, as we played barefoot, he would collapse in an epileptic fit.

In the center of the open courtyard was a scientifically designed structure called "Veedi". It was an octagonal 18-inch-high concrete platform with a corrugated pointed umbrella roof, supported with eight metal girders, and no side walls. In the center of the platform was a two-foot square, and two-foot deep, upside-down-pyramid-like concrete tank. Morning and evening rituals were a havan (prayer in the presence of the fire) with burning kindles, sprinkled on with mixed dry herbs and ghee (purified butter). The roof had a small opening in the middle of the umbrella shape to allow the herbal smoke to spread upwards and outwards and purify the surrounding air.

Our daily routine began with a 5am wake-up to the sound of banging on a thick brass plate by one student on the duty Rota. The power generator would be turned "On". I would hear a prayer from all the rooms in sync. They allocated an hour to brush our teeth with a twig of a particular thorny plant. After that we would begin grueling exercises conducted barefoot on an open ground, both in winter and summer. Once that was done it was time for a cold shower and to get ready for the lengthy prayer on the freezing floor of the "Veedi", the prayer platform in the center of the courtyard.

At 7am we queued up and marched to the canteen, for a breakfast comprising an enormous cup of warm milk and if we were lucky, one or two chapattis left over from the previous night.

Lunch was at 11am and then school from 12pm until 5pm. After the sports, shower, hour-long prayer and then a long day of schoolwork, we had our well-earned evening meal. They expected studies and homework were done until 8.45pm, then gave us were a few minutes for our evening prayers in bed before they turned the power generator "Off", a signal to go to bed.

On the sports field cricket was the city boys' game, whereas the much fitter village boys dominated football and wrestling. There was rivalry between us, but with the inter-school competitions, the comradeship brought us lots of winning trophies.

One year later I moved to the left-hand side of the Archway, going clockwise to the 8th standard. Ganeshji was our teacher for the 8th and 9th standards. We would carry on moving clockwise, going up the standards. For the 10th and 11th final years, Shyamdevji Sharma was our teacher. He was a brilliant football and volleyball player, and a scholar in Sanskrit.

As seniors we had the privilege to be in a five-bed dorm, a compact square room in the center of the north side of the building. Five of us were in the top ten students. Ramesh, Girish, Samlaji, Sudhir and myself. We always competed to be the top in most subjects.

"GURUKUL VIDYA MANDIR" GURUKUL SUPA

S. S. C. CLASS (1964-65)

From left : on chairs :-(1) B.B. Mori, (2) shri J. N. panchal (3) Shri H.S. Patel, (4) Shri R. D. Bhakta, (5) Shri K.R. Patel (6) Shri K.J Trivedi (Principal), (7) Shri Shashtriji (Mukhyadhisthata) (8) Shri W.N. Arya, (9) Shri S.T. Singh, (10) Shri H.G. Das (11) Shri H.R. Patel (12) Shri H.R. Mehta, (13) Shri S. C. Patel.
On Ground : (1) R.L. Patel, (2) H.S. Rathod, (3) M.K. Patel (4) H. H. patel, (5) M.B. Patel.
1st Row:(1) R. J. Patel, (2) J. V. Patel, (3) S. K. Patel, (4) J.R. Rathod, (5) K. P. Patel, (6) K. D. Goswami, (7) D.N. patel, (8) J. S. Patel, (9) K.N. Pandya, (10) H. P. Patel, (11) D.R. Bakta, (12) C. M. Ahir, (13) D. M. Desai.
2nd Row : (1) J. D. Karia, (2) C. K. Ahir, (3) H. M. Pandya, (4) S.D. Thaker, (5) A.N. Patel, (6) U.S. Amin, (7) U.H. Desai, (8) A.R. Patel,
Peon Shri Chhotubhai.

WELDON ART STUDIO NAVSARI.

A separate one-storey building, walking distance from the living accommodation, was for our academic studies. The junior and senior students were on separate floors. The school bell, a thick metal, brass plate, hung from the ceiling in the semi-circled gallery at the center of the first floor. A peon would sound the bell once every hour, signaling a period change. From the start to the end of school time, they would sound the bell continuously for half a minute, for each period.

On the front of the building was a flag mast on a small platform. They carried the raising of the Indian flag ceremony on 26th January,

India's Republic Day, and 15<sup>th</sup> August, India's Independence Day. A patriotic lecture would follow this by the head of the school or a visiting dignitary.

Mr. Satyavirji Patel, the math teacher, blessed with an extra thumb on both hands. Mr. Keshavji Trivedi, the principle was the only one in our school, standing straight, whose fingers tips would touch the bottom of his knees. He reminded me of Mahatma Gandhi, who also had long hands. Mr. Shyamdevji Sharma, in the rainy season, could kick a wet leather football (tied with leather string) from one end of the pitch to the other end, with his bare feet.

The dining area was another large single-storey square building which had tall and narrow rows of windows, with full-length metal bars. The kitchen, on the far side, had three enormous log fires. Food for 200 students prepared twice a day. Hundred students would sit cross-legged on a long plank laid on the floor. Students had their own brass drinking glass and a bowl. The school provided metal Thali (a round metal plate) to everyone. A team of students would serve meals on a monthly rota. They give every Sunday a treat, a sweet dish. While there was no restriction on the amount of food you could have, they took seriously any food wastage and came with a harsh punishment.

About 150 yards from the dormitory building, were a row of squatting toilets.

(*The squatting posture can ease problems like hemorrhoids*).

They stored the cleaning and flushing water in a large ground level concrete tank. There was a very basic drainage system. To divert the waste as fertiliser, make-shift open channels were dug into the woods and into the arable land, which was already fertile.

At night time we had a choice, we could either walk the length of a football pitch with a lantern to use the toilets, or we could go squatting in the nearby field of peanut plants and tall sugar canes. We were always on edge, looking out for sneaky snakes and slimy frogs. You had to be prepared to jump up from a squatting position. A bite from big red ants or a scorpion was painful.

Reciting "Hanuman Chalisa" gave us a bit of courage in the dark.

Teachers with families had free accommodation but had to share balconies or corridors, they also had shared toilets in a separate building. Bathing, cooking and washing done outside under the makeshift sheds.

 The general office, reception and the guest house were in another detached building. Establishment provided free accommodation and meals to visiting parents. They considered any donations from the parents a blessing.

 The bathing area was in a long shed with corrugated metal side walls. Along the length of the shed, in the center, was a water storage tank. They pumped water out early in the morning, from the deep well. It was warmer than the tap water, a blessing for the students in winter.

A small bucket or a container used to scoop water to pour over yourself. Normal practice was to bathe with underpants on. 20 to 25 students on the both sides of the long tank would bathe at a time. The water tank similar to the herd drinking lengthy trough.

Gurukul had its own power generator in the stand-alone building. They turned it "On" and "Off" at a set times, in the morning and evening. Only the senior students could study with lanterns after hours, after they turned the generator "Off".

Students played and learned football, hockey, cricket, or volleyball. We played most of the games barefooted. It was challenging to play with a water-soaked leather football in the rain, in the muddy field, with bare feet. The leather lace left lethal lines on our feet.

Some of us preferred to take up playing musical instruments or singing lessons taught by Ratanjibhai. He was blind from birth, strict with a stick, but a magical music master.

Running and grueling exercises in the morning were compulsory all year round and it all had to be done barefoot.

For me, it was a joy to dress up in the ACC khaki uniform and give orders to the marching parade. I was the captain, without the badge. A leader without a portfolio. From a young age, the uniforms had always impressed me, be it Army, Air force, Navy, or ACC (Army cadet corps, India).
During the scorching summers, the river Purna dried up into a stream, making it safer for splashing and swimming under supervision. Local farm workers planted watermelons along the edge of the stream in the fertile mud. It was childish fun to steal the sweet fruit.

At night time when the generator turned "Off", a team of four or five of us would venture out. We would strategically stand around the coconut tree on lookout duty, one would climb the tree. He would drop coconuts down into the hedges to muffle the sounds.

The lookout scouts would warn others with a flashlight, if anyone spotted a wandering teacher or caretaker.

The five of us the seniors, had an advantage. We had easy access in the night to the field full of fully grown, juicy sugar canes, peanut plants, and the trees full of big mangos.

One summer evening, while playing volleyball we were disturbed. We heard shouts, a frantic cry from the direction of the dried riverbed. We couldn't see, but we heard someone calling us, as the riverbed was quite a lot lower than the playing field. The shout was familiar; it was that of an elderly teacher we knew. We ran towards the river. There was a sweaty, red-faced teacher in his 50s coming towards us. He was huffing, puffing and couldn't spell out, whatever he was trying to tell us. He just mumbled, pointing in the river's direction. There was fear in his eyes. He said something like there were three boys in the water.

He must have run an interminable distance on the sand.

We ran towards the water. There was no sign of the boys. We looked at each other with panic in our eyes. Two of us stayed with the teacher to calm him down and to get some sense out of him. Three of us, the best swimmers, walked in the shallow water. We only paddled in about two feet, then suddenly there was a drop of seven or eight feet. We all felt the sudden fear of drowning. After a few minutes struggle and searching, we found the boys. We grabbed all three lifeless children. We tried to revive them and gave basic first aid by slapping their backs while holding them high by the ankles. Unfortunately, none of us had CPR training.

It was hopeless. Their bodies remained lifeless. It was decision time. The only choice was to carry their bodies to the medical center.

They called the doctors in from the nearby village, as there was no resident doctor. He pronounced all three of them dead.

It was a shocking coincidence that all three boys came from the same class; they were the only children in their families and all three sets of parents wouldn't be able to reach the school within a day.

They volunteered me to assist the compounder. To dress and lay their bodies on ice in order to preserve them for the next 24 hours.

One boy had his mouth open and was full with mud.

Who would remove the mud and close the mouth?

Would the jaws snap-shut by themselves?

The generator was already powered down, ready for sleep. That night seemed darker than the darkest night. The lantern's dim flickering light cast eerie shadows. A chill felt in the air and the ghostly sound of falling dead twigs on the metal roof sent shivers down my spine. It terrified us. We stayed closed to each other, trying not to show weakness.

The dead bodies' pale crinkly yellowish soft skin would peel off to the touch. Their ears dripped fluid onto the white sheet, it had the stench of rotten fish.

As I tried to dress one child, the entire body stood up. Shaken by the unexpectedly stiff corpse, I dropped it on the ice, jumped back, and knocked over the compounder. My forehead sweating in chilled air, and heart pumping faster than a sprinter's. Thumping was disturbing in the deadly darkness. The tiny hairs on my bare arms stood up like the prickles on a defensive hedgehog.

The shirt I was gripping with both hands suddenly waved, and I dropped it. I screamed and leapt back again. Was the shirt alive? Staring at the body and then the shirt and then the body, I stood stunned and sweating in the light breeze.

Teacher, never told us that the dead body's joints would weld together.

Even the compounder was taken aback with my sudden jerking, dropping the body, and then the shirt. He was also breathing in and out through his open mouth and his eyes were wide open. He nearly had heart attack, he cursed me for frightening him.

That was the longest night I have ever experienced.

The cow shed with 40 healthy cows was far on the north side of our accommodation. Each cow had its own name. Enough milk produced to feed the entire school. It was fascinating to see cow breeds from all over Gujarat. Gurukul had Gir cows, rated among the best dairy breed in the world. While learning about the animal husbandry, it was fun to play with the cuddly young calves.

After graduation of the 11th standard, they took group photo with the teachers and the peon.

We exchanged addresses, so we could write to each other. Mobile phones were a thing of science fiction then.

We all departed in different directions, heading to different cities with our own families. We all had original dreams and different priorities. Some kept in touch, others were forgotten. Some climbed the work ladder while others were happy where they were.

Satish D H Thaker

# 4 BHAVAN'S COLLEGE 1ST YR SCIENCE

After lots of struggles, recommendations, and paying the donation, I got the admission into the 1st year science, at the Bhavan's College, Andheri (West). The college was next to my previous day school, a half -hour bus ride from the Vile Parle (West), where I stayed with my mum. Dad was still in Aden, trying to make ends meet. My elder brother, Jitendra, had started a joint venture, saree dying/printing factory in Vapi, near Daman. My two younger brothers were at the Gurukul-Supa.

The year which followed at Bhavans College, was just a year of experience, it wasn't very productive. The lecture rooms were three to four times larger than the one at the Gurukul-Supa. There was a lack of discipline. Students came to the class as they pleased, in their own time. The first few weeks felt uneasy, sharing a lecture room, and competing with the girls. The students weren't serious enough, and there was no accountability. I was drifting away, and didn't know the purpose of being there. Totally confused, I had my head in the sand. I can't recall having any college friends. There were too many distractions, and nothing to motivate me.

Despite all this, I had a proud moment, when I wore the Green Beret with the feather behind the shiny brass badge and starched ironed NCC (National Cadet Corps) uniform. I enjoyed an experience on the firing range, getting to fire a Lee Enfield 303 rifle. My eyesight wasn't good enough to be a marksman, though.

An incidence I'll never forget, when I was in a comedy play. One part of the act in particular, sticks in my mind. In the play an overly sensitive class girl slap me with a chapel (a pair of slippers), as I tried flirting with her. Then I got kicked by a teacher, who was her overprotective dad. The irony is that after one of the evening rehearsals, the girl's real-life, overprotective brother was watching the play. He took it too seriously and beat me up outside the college gate.

I dreamed of being an actor. I auditioned to be in a scene set on a battlefield; I was a doctor attending the wounded soldiers. My acting wasn't too bad for a newcomer. After the audition, reality unfolded though. It was a daylight scam. They demanded a bribe. Unfortunately, I didn't have it. A blessings in disguise. That was the end of acting for me.

At the end of the college academic year I failed. I had failed the 1st year. Enough was enough. I packed-up. I had no desire to study. The future was bleak, I couldn't face it.

I couldn't get hung up on anymore.

I knew I had the power to rewrite and change the situation.

I decided that I would help and learn dad's business in Aden. He had many years of experience buying and selling under his belt. His friends said that he could sell a fur coat to the Bedouins.

# 5 BACK ON THE STEAMER

The steamer was at full speed ahead. I wasn't sure if I had made the right decision. There was no turning back now, though. I had to take life as it came. I knew dad for his strict beliefs of excellent education. At a young age it threw him in the deep end, by having to look after his siblings and elders.

He had high expectations of me; he presumed my school reports were exemplary.

It was getting dark and chilly on the top upper deck, so I came down to the lower deck. The lights were dim. The passengers tucked away under their sheets. A few were leaning over to chat to their neighbors below. They gave me a quick glance and smiled. I noticed they chained the metal trunks to their metal beds sides. There were around 50 bunk beds, all occupied. My bed was the upper bunk. The lower beds were more popular, someone to grab first. From there you could monitor your belongings. The lower beds were also easier for the elderly to roll in and out of.

There was no shower room and only five toilets to share between hundreds of us, of all shapes and sizes.

Using loo roll was an enormous surprise for me. A single layer loo paper was like a newspaper, hardly absorbent and will float when flushed down the loo.

In the first instant it sounded disgusting - wiping your back side with the paper!

I'd seen dogs and cats sliding on the grass with their hind legs folded after they have pooped, and this didn't seem so different! Occasionally at the boarding school, I used the riverbed mud to wipe my back-end and then jumped in the river for a full wash. I never imagined using toilet paper.

The boarding school taught me the phrase early to bed, early to rise literally. I followed the daily ritual before the sunrise, and before others queued up.

The sunshine was spectacular with a clear sky. The sea turned light green, somewhat different from when we left Bombay. It was calm with the light ripple of waves in the distance. The frothy trail still followed us.

During the daytime, schools of fish were more visible. They stayed with us, hoping for the scraps and leftovers from the kitchen. It spoiled the fish; they expected food from spectators on the deck. As the school of fish got bigger and bigger, spectators piled up on the deck to watch them.

It was a fresh day. Another day, new friends, and something new to learn.

I met Sudhir (not his actual name), a Gujarati boy. He was a year older than I was. It was odd that he was going back to Aden, with his mother, aunt, and uncle. Odd because most Gujarati ladies left Aden to be safe away from the conflict.

Sudhir and I explored the steamer together, we played cards and table tennis. We became best friends, even sharing our secrets.

One day, he took me to the side, and with an air of secrecy he gave me this book with a condition - not to mention it to anybody and to be discrete. It was a special book of knowledge, in Hindi.

A special book!!!

It piqued my curiosity!

I didn't want to be left out, "the special book of knowledge"? I was excited and intrigued.

I had to find a place quickly where I could read without being disturbed or caught.

My curiosity was killing me.

I didn't want to miss the chance or the privilege of reading this book.

I wouldn't be able to read in bed. There was no table light and no privacy. I was sharing the bunk bed in an enormous hall with a sizeable group of mainly elders.

Few people used the kitchen, especially not nosy ladies. I was lucky to have verbal permission to go to the kitchen any time.

That was it.

The kitchen crew were illiterates. They only spoke Urdu and understood spoken Hindi. The special book was in Hindi. Hooray! I had found my hiding place.

The book was the "Kama-Sutra".

It made me wonder what is "Kama-Sutra" ?

I was fluent in Hindi, but I had never heard of "Kama-Sutra". But what an exciting name. I was hesitant but pressed on. As I read, my excited mind was getting more adventurous. I felt so guilty, but I felt liberated.

I soon realised why all the secrecy was necessary. It was in my interest not to be careless. He trusted me, only me. What a privilege!

I admit I was enjoying the science of the "Kama-Sutra".

I couldn't imagine what would happen If they caught me reading the "Kama-Sutra". They disapproved it of; they would alienate me. And if someone told Sudhir's dad, no doubt my dad would come to know too.

Was I ready to face the guilt and shame and maybe punishment?

It was a challenging predicament.

I took my chances though and read on. It was time for an adventure

# 6 HERE I COME ADEN

*Granddad Harjeevanlal and Grandma Santokba, the pioneers to settle in Aden*

A fleet of fishing boats appeared in the distance as we came nearer to Aden, in the Gulf of Aden. The Arabian Sea was rich with a variety of exotic fish.

It was the early morning of 23rd April 1966.

There were still a few hours before the scorching sun would reach noon. The coastline was on the horizon. The "Small Ben", Aden's landmark and the beacon for ships approaching the harbor, was just about visible

*The "Small Ben" a replica of "Big Ben" in Parliament Square, London*

The steamer anchored about half a mile from the "Steamer Point" Dock, in Tawahi.

My metal trunk was ready and packed. It had travelled with me to and from boarding schools. It had been a suitable companion, and a useful seat on packed train journeys.

The customs officials came on board for the immigration formalities. Most of the officials were Parsees and English. All the passengers were eager to leave the floating 2* hotel. It was nerve-racking to descend via the wobbly and narrow metal stairs hanging from the crane to the transfer boat waiting to take us to the shore. Fortunately, the Arabian Sea was calm.

The distinct rusty smell of the metal stairs mixed with the salty seawater brought back memories of my childhood in Aden.

Dad had organised boating trips around the coast. I looked forward to the rare treats of white baps, with butter and English cheese. Dad's friend, the immigration officer, when on duty, bought the English white bread loaf and cheese as a favor.

It had been three years since I had last seen my dad; it seemed a long time. My mind was full of questions, my stomach churning.

What would his reaction be?

Would he be angry or sorry for me for failing the first year of college?

Would he hug me or frown at me?

It was the first time I had failed any exams, and it was disturbing to me. I was angry and worried. The college environment, the distraction of flirting boys and girls, and the freedom I had never had before was the perfect recipe for disaster.

The punishment would be harsh, but only verbally, that I knew.

As the boat came near to the shore, there he was, a tall handsome fellow in his milky white shirt, light coloured trousers and dark sunglasses. He gave me a smile and a nod, helping me to feel at ease. I dived off the boat, nearly slipped, and ran into his arms.

A hug from my hero.

**My dad** (Late *Dhirajlal H Thaker*)

I admired him; I respected him a lot, but the fear, the fear of my failure was killing me.

'Hi Dhirubhai, kem cho! How are you?'

Dad's Parsee friend asked, 'He is not your dikro, is he?' pointing at me.

My dad nodded, 'Yes, he is my son.'

'Dikra…bolavo joyene, you should have said, I would have placed you in the first-class spare cabin. Biji var, next time talk to me. I am always travelling from Aden to Bombay and back.'

That reassured me that next time I wouldn't have to spend days on the lower deck, sleeping on the metal bunk bed.

Aden was one of the busiest bunkering ports in the world during the period of 1959 -1965. Aden was strategically placed to service ships passing through the Suez Canal and the Red Sea. Vessels of all nationalities and classes including cargo, passenger, and naval ships with their auxiliary support ships were all frequent callers.

Aden was a tax-free shopper's paradise and there seemed to be plenty of choice when window-shopping or if you were looking to purchase from the many shops in the Crescent (Tawahi). The Crescent was within short walking distance of the Prince of Wales Pier, where passengers and crew from visiting ships would disembark during their stay in port to shop from the local amenities. You could get cameras and binoculars from The Popular Stores or the Camera Craft. Transistor radios and Rolex watches could be purchased from the Reliance Stores. Travel bags and ladies' purses bought from the Majestic. To the top of the range of clothing and jewelry, there were shops catering to every possible need of visitors and residents alike.

The local fruit and veg markets, made popular by the Indians, stocked an excellent range of fresh vegetables exported from East Africa. Thanks to the Indians for introducing vegetables in Aden. During the early settlement, the local Arabs and the Somalian staple diet was chicken and goat meat. The British Forces families relied on processed tinned foods and were happy with the English beer. Local bakeries and food shops provided a wide range of meat and luxury foods either shipped or flown in from across the world for the local civilians and the armed forces families.

There was plenty of supply of reconstituted milk, a long-life milk.

They pumped the water supply up from deep wells. The pumped-up water supply soon ran hot, as the sun would heat the metal storage tanks on the terraces and the piping system during the day.

Tawahi, known as Steamer Point during the British Colonial period, had a straight road running between Tawahi and the Crater Pass known as "The Ma'alla Straight". It was a long straight road built with large blocks of flats along it to house the married service families, with local shops, a petrol station and café-style restaurants.

BP, British Petroleum, built the oil refinery and the tanker port in Little Aden.

# 7 BEGINNING OF A NEW FUTURE

The searing sun at 12 o'clock was enough to make my skin burn red and my face sticky with dried sweat. We went straight to Laban

Galli, to our 1st floor corner flat situated on a T-junction. There was an Arab café on the ground floor. On the other corner of the Laban Galli, was an Arab owned grocery shop. Culturally, only men or kids would shop. Unlike a "Patel's Corner Shop" in the UK, it hardly stored anything.

A popular "Paanwala", beside cigarettes, matches, long canes and boiled sweets, was selling tambul or Paan, a green leaf spread with brown sweat paste and grated coconut with chopped betel nuts.

Indians brought the Paan eating tradition to Aden, along with their outfits, curry and the Jalabi, the sweet.

The Paanwala sold more metre long canes, than the Paan. The cane to keep away the venturing nuisance goats that were fouling the ground with their black marble-like droppings. A long cane was also a handy tool for parents, especially for father who needed to control their uncontrollable kids. It was an excuse to relieve their bottled-up frustration and anger.

(Paan is originally from and native to India / Pakistan.)

*Sanu & Arun on the terrace in front of the metal Water tanks*

*Note: The black water tank, which stored sun heated water, was an ideal position to sit on and watch movies screened from the open-air theatre in Tawahi.*

I showered in the scorching tap water, piped from the metal tank on top of the flat roof. Being back at the flat, brought back many memories. The dining area in our flat reminded me of one particular childhood incident. Vinod, my cousin, and I were playing in the dining area. My grandma let out a big fart as she had forgotten that we were there. We looked at each other and burst into laughter. Vinod couldn't stop laughing, with his distinctive high-pitched hissing laugh. I tried to control myself but couldn't. Grandma told us to stop, I did for a moment, but Vinod couldn't. Every few minutes he would start again. That was it. Grandma was furious. When dad came home from the shop, grandma exaggerated and complained that we had been very naughty.

Dad was furious.

He couldn't stand his mum being insulted at any cost. Soon he grabbed the metre long cane and started swinging it in all directions. We were screaming with pain, trying to avoid the blows, running around grandma. With all that anger dad couldn't control his swing, he missed Vinod and hit grandma.

Then she knew what it was like to be caned.

Grandma never complained again.

I didn't have long to reminisce though. After a quick change we went to my elder uncle Vajubapa's Dharmshala, for lunch. It was a meeting point for the Thakers, most often for a meal. Especially when the ladies were away to India.

Every Thursday the Thakers gathered for bhajans and prayers, and to socialise. Uncle would cook mouth-watering spaghettis with a touch of Indian flavor.

It was fun to fetch French Sticks from the bakery behind the Dharmasala. The man with his feet knee-deep, did dough kneading. French breads were mouth-watering. Uncle gave each of us a tin of melted "Kenya Butter" to dunk the warm bread in, a weekly treat.

The Dharamshala was just behind the police station. The Steamer Point police station appeared impressive from the front. The cells were out of sight at the rear. There was a wall around it between the cells. The police would eat their food whilst Arab prisoners watched, they were teasing the prisoners while they were half starved. They fed them with the leftover scraps. The cells were merely a concrete cube, no water, no TV, no toilet. The cells washed out every morning by an Arab policeman with a fire hose. It was not pleasant to any standard.

From the first floor of the verandas we could see the backyard and the cells. The police caned screaming prisoners with a cane in each hand.

*Opposite Prince of Wales Pier, the former Tawahi Police Station*

Aswad, an Arab orphan, trained as a cook from a young age at the Dharmasala, which was his home. He spoke Gujarati and adopted Hindu culture, enjoyed attending religious festivals and vegetarian cooking. He became a part of uncle's family.

*Uncle: Vrajlal (Vajubhai) Harjivanlal Thaker*

The short-term workers and travelers frequently visited Dharmshala, on transit from India and Africa. It was the only place in Tawahi for pure vegetarian Hindu meals and accommodation at reasonable rates. Sunday was feast-day. At lunch uncle served, specially cooked Indian sweets with the main meal. It was popular amongst the British Forces and their families. He enjoyed being the cook and a waiter. He served his customers and would insist that they ate as much as they could, at a set price. His pleasure was the customer's satisfaction. He wasn't business minded, just a down to earth, gentle giant, and a good cook. In his twenties, Uncle was a wrestler, he was so strong that he could split a metal pot in half. He would carry large sacks of potatoes for miles without a rest.

He would insist upon taking the milk delivery personally every day and would check the water content once in a while. One particular day, it was unwelcome news for the milkman. He tried his luck once too often and added too much water to the milk. Uncle enraged, poured 8 litres of milk over the milkman, and slammed the container on his head. The milkman shivered, shaking with fear. He never tried that trick again.

My dad with his younger brother Ishwarlal (Babubhai)

**The first shop we bought was the Popular Store**

*My dad and Manubhai Vakharia with the directors of Cannon Camera*

Early every morning Uncle Vajubhai walked four miles to the Shree Ram-Mandir, the community temple, built in 1875. It was the only Hindu temple in Tawahi. My other uncle Amubhai, would attend in the evening, for the evening prayers. Thakers took a dual role of both the trustees and the caretakers.

My dad and uncles, Bhogibhai, Pravinbhai and Babubhai visited the temple on Saturdays or Sundays. Occasionally we all visited the temple on the same day and made it an outing. The British Army barracks was next to the temple, it acted as a deterrent from any intrusions and made it secure.

During my childhood I spent a lot of time at the Ram-Mandir. We celebrated the Hindu festivals at the temple. Within the temple there were three separate shrines. Ram, Sita, Laxman and Hanumanji in one. Radha-Krishan in the second, and Shiv-linga and Nanadi in the third shrine. As our parents were the trustees, they allowed us inside the shrines. The children collected the coins offered by the devotees during the festival prayers. To round up and collect a mountain of copper coins was exhilarating. During the festival of Shiv-Ratri, hundreds of Hindus would visit the temple, especially to drink bhang, a mixer of milk, water and Ganja. A small concrete water tank in the corner was an attraction for the youngsters to jump in and splash about. We fought for our turns, as the tank was big enough to take two.

There were two matured trees, one sweet and one bitter Limdo. The sweet Limdo, curry leaves used in Indian cooking and we used other one for home remedies. Once a month dad forced us to drink the bitter juice. It tasted awful, but it cleared the system. There was a fruit tree of Vilaiti-amli (foreign-Amli), which can be mistaken as a peapod, the fruit turned pink when it was ripe. We use sour Amli (Tamarind) grown in India for cooking.

As a young boy, I enjoyed watching the runway activities, such as the Westland Whirlwind helicopters on their daily aerial patrol, at RAF Khormaksar. The road to the Sheikh Othman was through Check Point Charlie via Lake Lines. The Beach Road was leading to the Abyan beach.

The British Army, Navy and Air force troops deployed to Redfan Mountain, it was a priority task to stabilise the region.

Aden was a popular place for those going on a shopping spree for German cameras and then years later Japanese cameras too. It was one of the best free ports during the late 50s and early 60s. There was no restriction on business opening hours. The passenger ships arriving from Europe, docking at 2 o'clock in the morning would be a bonus. The shops in Tawahi, Steamer Point, would be open for business for an hour. That's if the visitors were from Europe and not from Russia or China. The Europeans were good spenders, while the others had little to spend.

By 1966 we had four shops under the Thaker's banner. The first two were Reliance & Popular Stores. Both stores were selling German Cameras, Kodak films, Rolex and Omega watches, Parker pens, and so on. In the early 50s, German cameras were the most popular. In the 60s Japanese cameras dominated the market. Japanese cameras were cheaper, compact and took more photos with a single film roll. The Parker pen was a prestigious item to have or to gift to someone special. Chinese "Paker" pen (without the 1st 'r'), appeared to be an exact replica of the famous 'Parker' pen, which came to the market in the early 1960's. It was cheap but useless.

Around 1967, the Thaker families moved to India. As they matured and realised that the future in India would be challenge, the cousins and nieces came to the UK.

The Patira and Vakharia family also moved to India and settled in Bombay and Rajkot, as they were financially stable.

The Khimji, Shrimanker, Depala families who had little connection to India, made their future in the UK.

In my youth, standing outside our shop, Camera Crafts, we called Europeans by popular names, Jakes, James or Pedro and Amigos to invite them into the shop.

British soldiers in their uniform looked smart and handsome with their machine guns and communication gadgets. Some had dark tans and others looked like fresh pink lobsters.

In the boarding school, I always admired English and Australian cricketers. Often, I tried to mimic the cricket commentators.

My roommate Ramesh's dad Lalbhai was in England. Ramesh always showed me the photos from England.

We well knew English and German engineering achievements were the best. Although we heard a lot about atrocities committed by British rulers in India, no seeds of hate were planted against the British Raj by our teachers. They taught us to be tolerant and be like a sponge, to learn additional things when it was to do with education.

Besides a few nasty incidences between Arabs and Jews, everybody lived in peace and harmony.

As someone said, 'Life is full of possibilities. The only things that matter is who you want to be and where you want to be'.

Childhood dreams were endless, but as we grew older, some of those dreams remained unexplored due to the fear of failure. And that is true for most of us.

Childhood in Aden in the 1950s was interesting. Every day was an adventure. The last Sunday of the month was hair cut day. Dad left me and Sanu, my younger brother, at the Bachubhai barber's shop next to the Dharmasala. It was the only Indian barber shop in Tawahi. His shop was four feet above the road level, with a large steppingstone to the door. Sanu, as usual, was in his mischievous mood.

While waiting for our cuts, we were messing around, having fun. We were just playing with a plastic ball; he took it out of my hand. I ran after him to get it back. He ran straight towards the entrance, tripped and somersaulted onto the road. As he fell his right ankle landed in a small pothole. It took the wind out of me. A passing car took a big chunk out of his foot below the ankle joint. Soon the pothole was full of thick blood.

Really it was a blessing in disguise, the pothole had saved his ankle from being crushed under the wheel.

I cried; it was my fault. I was the elder, I should have controlled him. I thought he was going to die. I would get all the blame and the punishment.

It wasn't the punishment I was crying for though; it was the guilt. Thankfully Sanu was OK and only had some scars on his foot afterwards.

I spent the first day with my dad, at our shop, The Popular Store. I met Mr. Kadarbhai Rangonwala a Muslim-khoja, father's business partner. He had family connections in India and in Pakistan.

He was one of the influential figures in my destiny.

Late 50s, Kadarbhai suffered a tragic accident. He was driving from Tawahi to Ma'lla (one suburb), with dad in the passenger seat. At the road junction, he indicated right, with his hand stretched out (in the 50s hand signals were in use) an over-taking speeding car took his hand, right off from the elbow.

There was no time to wait for an ambulance or for the police. His best friend's life was in his own hands. The clock was ticking. He had to move faster than the speed of light. He wrapped the sheared hand in a rag, jumped behind the wheel and raced through the traffic lights with no regard for the law.

He couldn't believe his quick thinking and the action he took.

What makes people break the barriers, break the rules, and overcome obstacles to get to the finishing line? There is no point worrying when time is of the essence. Sometimes people need to raise to that level more often to achieve the impossible.

The doctors saved his life, not his detached arm. Their friendship flourished. They were like two brothers from two different religions. Kadarbhai's wife Sugraben and my mum regularly organised early morning picnics to farms to drink palm water and late evening trips for boat rides. Their daughter Nargis and son Rafi called my dad Dhiru-kaka and my mum Manu-masi. In 1967, because of their family connection, they moved to Pakistan. Nargis studied medicine in Dundee, Scotland.

After the dinner at the Dharmshala, we went back to the flat. It was a one-bedroom flat with a lounge and a collection of seven windows on the longer side and two windows on the narrow side. There was a large "Grunding" TV at the far end, a sign of luxury. A recliner, a side table and a chair set-up to watch the TV from a safe distance. At the other end of the room was a Godrej metal cabinet with a mirror on one door. The cabinet doors were covered with a net. The lounge seemed like a badminton court, as there was no other furniture.

We had meals sitting on the floor in front of the kitchen. The compact kitchen had a concrete worktop and built-in sink. A double ring portable gas burner attached to a gas cylinder for cooking.

Next to the kitchen was a walk-in shower with a 24/7 heated water supply and an adjoining toilet with a high platform (unlike the floor level) with a built-in squatting toilet. As a young boy, I would eat chocolate in the toilet, undisturbed.

A few inches high concrete wall, designated as the low-level washing square for clothes or to wash pots and pans. A large Somalian lady would squat down for hours to do her daily chores here.

In the nights, the lounge floor used as a bedroom. It was fun to roll all over the floor on futons.

There were two entry doors and stairs to the flat. The entrance from the Laban Galli was the main door, in use by us, the milkman, and uncle's family on the 2nd floor. If the door left unlocked at night, the goats would climb up the stairs and curl-up on the steps. Although the goat's black droppings didn't smell, they were slippery, so it was unwise to leave them on the stairs. The goats were dumb but challenging to get rid of. A docile animal, but a nuisance as it would climb up the parked cars to sleep, leaving scratches and dents on the bonnet and the car roof top.

That evening we watched the Western series 'Bonanza' in Arabic with English subtitles. Neither of us followed the story, just the gunfight.

We sat in silence, watching the box. One of us had to break the ice. I felt like there was a sword hanging over my neck and it would drop any moment. The topic I dreaded was my college results.

After a few minutes that felt like an hour, Dad asked me to turn the volume down so that he could talk.

With a very serious expression, no anger, he looked at me, straight to the point, he asked me, 'What happened?'

'An entire year's money...... down the drain!'

He continued, 'Look at me, tell me what happened?'

I presumed he was referring to my exam results.

What could I say? He was right, I had let him down.

I sat in silence, with my head down, staring at the floor with guilt.

Dad believed in an excellent education as he missed out. At a young age, he was thrown in the deep end by having to look after his siblings and some elders. He wanted to fulfil his dream through me and my brothers.

I dared not speak or else. I glanced at him. There was no anger on his face, just sadness. He was in deep thought. Maybe he was drawing, predicting my future. He knew there was no future in Aden. There was a strong rumour that the British would leave, soon. He knew that with no education, there was no future. His vision was big.

The silence was deafening.

Suddenly there was the *bang-bang,* two hand-grenades going off, followed by gunfire and the screeching stop of military jeeps and sirens. The windows became alive with flashing lights. All I could hear was the commotion along with screams of pain.

As I jumped up from sitting, dad pulled me down, back onto the chair. My curiosity would have killed me. The sudden opening of a window would have ended up with me getting shot. It was a first-hand experience of live action.

The freedom movement was in full swing. The sound of hand grenades exploding every few minutes, followed by gunfire and sirens, was the norm.

At the end of the British supremacy when they departed in 1967, it left Aden in a deep black hole. The blood thirsty power struggles between fanatics was on the rise, but it was unorganized and uncontrollable.

Sadly, Aden was tearing apart between the civilised and uncivilised culture.

In 2020, the wounds have only been dug deeper and wider. There is no stopping to it. The Adenians are wounded inside and out. Their heritage is in ruins. Hope is nowhere in sight; any changes would be the miracle of the century.

Where had the brotherhood gone?

What changed?

Where did the fanatics spring up from?

The religious fanatics, the extremists, and the self-centred egomaniacs causing atrocities in the name of religion - aren't they the weeds of the society?

After a lengthy silence, dad got up and pulled out two wrist watches from a drawer in the side cabinet. He placed them in front of me and asked me to choose one. After a bit of hesitation, I picked the Rolex. Why the Rolex? I still don't know. But I did. And now what I thought then was the right decision, at the time. I don't want to guess what would have happened if I had picked the other watch.

He looked straight in my eyes and said, 'Do you want to go to England for further studies?'

It shocked me, I couldn't believe what I was hearing.

I couldn't imagine why? Perhaps I will never know.

He asked me again, 'Do you want to go to England, yes or no?'

I suddenly woke up, 'Yes!' Shaking my head a few times.

Opportunity was knocking on my door!

I still couldn't believe my luck.

He had higher expectations of me as he wanted to fulfil his dreams through me.

After a brief silence, dad spoke, 'Ok, start preparing from tomorrow. I have arranged for you to attend tuition classes in English, math, typewriting and shorthand. You have two months to prepare.'

He stopped for a while to think, and then added, 'and the most important thing, tell no one, and that means no one, that you will go to England. Understand? Not even your mum should know about it until it is time to go.'

As mum was in Bombay, only dad and I were there. He knew that my mum could be very emotional and might hinder my immigrating to the UK.

The Indians thinking was that the Westerners were rich, clever, smart, and intelligent but morally, only a 2 out of 10. They were drunkards and behaved like animals in public. They would kiss and cuddle in front of their own children, parents, and strangers. No shame.

My mum had told me the saga, previously of what happened to

Vinod, my cousin.

Three years earlier, my dad had organised to send him to London for further studies. Vinod's parents were very reluctant but agreed.

As a family tradition, dad had to have a meeting with his four brothers to discuss this adventure of sending the first member of the Thaker family to London. There was a heated discussion and argument. The majority opposed the idea, except my dad and Vinod's dad.

*Young Vinod going to London and becoming independent?*

*No way.*

*No, we can't have that.*

*It will spoil him.*

*Who will stop him going out with English girls and getting drunk?*

*Oh no, it is completely out of question. He just can't go.*

*We can't afford to spoil his future. He will be out of our control.*

*That's it. No.*

They believed that England was not very good for our culture. The influence of English culture would spoil their child and would bring shame to our name. That was the thinking among the elders. Being an elder son, he had responsibilities to look after his younger brothers and sisters.

Often relatives and good wishers give advice and opinions, even when they lack the experience or any facts. They think they want to help, or some want to dominate, or they just want to express their views without thinking about the consequences.

That was what had happened in Vinod's case. Dad was all in favour and excited for Vinod to go to England.

But no, it didn't materialise because of others opinions on the matter.

Dad and Vinod's dreams, the journey to London, and further education, had all shattered. It had ended before it had even started.

My dad didn't want history to repeat with me. Hence, he asked me to keep it to myself.

Now I knew why my dad wanted to keep all under the carpet, until it has finalised. He wanted to avoid obstacles, arguments or any heated discussions. He had a vision for me. He had dreams.

Those dreams would soon be a reality.

*Youngest brother Raju, Abyan Beach*

**The sole agent of the Cannon Camera 'The Popular Stores' Tawahi**

*Uncle in Aden Police Academy*

*Grand-ma with Uncle and aunties*

*My Dad with uncle late Ishwarlal (Babubhai)*

 While I was preparing for the next leg of my journey, I met Mr. Shankarbahi (Kantibahi), dads' childhood friend and his wife Kantaben. She looked up to my dad as her elder brother. Shankarbhai and my dad had gone through ups and down in life, together.

He sold the German swimming costumes from a tiny shop next to RAF Khormakshar, where 35 Sqn of the Avro Shackleton, (British Long Range Maritime Patrol Aircraft) was based in 1960s

**Kantibhai with his dad and the extended family.**

Kantibahi's younger sister Kisanben, a qualified NHS nurse, was based at the Khormakshar British Forces hospital. After speaking to her, she convinced me going to the UK for further studies would be a splendid idea. It was straight from the horse's mouth.

Kishore Shrimankar my childhood friend from Aden. Luckily, I bumped into him in Aden while he was on vacation from the UK. He spoke highly about the education standard and life in London. He was another person who inspired and motivated me.

The day was drawing nearer. My passport was stamped, the reference letters prepared, and finance was sorted. Dad was going to support me financially. One evening, Dad took me to the Chinese restaurant, "Pagoda", to get a taste of Western etiquette.

Most important tip was to tilt the soup bowl away from the body to prevent accidental spillage on yourself. Traditionally, the fork held in left hand and the knife in your right. The soup was the starter, followed by the main meal and then the sweet dish. With the Indian custom, sweet was part of the main meal. He also told me that burping considered unpleasant manners in the weird Western world.

*Satish with Mr Kadarbhai Rangonwala*

*Satish ready to fly from Aden—1966*

I was eager and learning fast. Dad decided that I would travel with Kantibhai. The journey was planned so I would adapt to the culture and new traditions and acclimatise as I went along.

Finally, on the day of the departure, dad wanted me to observe TWO things in life:

*Everything you earn, is not all yours.*

*Not to do anything that will tarnish the Thakers' name.*

I didn't take much notice at the time; I was too excited.

I didn't know what he meant; it overwhelmed me.

I didn't know what it was all about.

I was full of excitement and eager to explore the world.

Eventually dad informed my uncles. Obviously, they weren't happy. However, they came to terms with it. I was their favorite nephew; they gave me lots of advice on what to do and what not to do.

I was too excited to take notice of any words of wisdom. ready to explore, starting with a blank page

Youngest Uncle with his childhood friend Dhirubhai Ambani (Ambani Groups.

Gatway to the Aden Crator

Satish D H Thaker

# 8 CAIRO, HERE I COME

*Kantibhai enjoying Shisha in Cairo*

**Satish Thaker at the footstep of Pyramid in Cairo**

Aden to Cairo was the first leg of my journey. The Hotel Cairo International, a four-storey building hidden behind a three-storey office block. The second floor of the office block was a mass tailoring enterprise. We were on the third floor, facing the office block.

Cairo was full of street foods and footpath cafes. My first taste of BBQ lamb chunks was mouth-watering, but it was a bit chewy for my liking. It was a rare treat cooked for the locals.

Every morning from my hotel windows I watched and waved to Kasim (not an actual name) on the third floor of the offices. Out of the windows I spoke at the top of my voice in broken Arabic-English, to get attention of the girls working on the sewing machines on the second floor.

Kasim's niece Nadia, a college student, worked part time on the second floor. When I mentioned that I was heading to UK, they both wanted to be my pen-friends.

Kasim invited me to the Cairo Stadium to celebrate 'The President Day'. Gamal Abdel Nasser was a very influential president to the Egyptian and the Arab world. *(Gamal Abdel Nasser Hussein was the second President of Egypt, serving from 1954 until his death in 1970.)*

 To my disappointment, Nadia could not to join us due to the cultural and religious restrictions. The gunfire, fireworks, the sequential military parade, music and dancing lasted for two hours.

The next day I was excited to be visiting the pyramids. Climbing the six-foot square stones in the scorching heat was an experience I will never forget. They lay stones on top of each other, cemented with just sand. The entrance to the inside of the hollow Pyramid was a hundred feet high, not even a quarter of the way to the top of the pyramid. The pyramid stood as the tallest structure in the world for over 4000 years.

With a few coins of baxis, the guide took me to the underground tomb. I had to lay on my back and slide down into the tomb. The dim lantern flickered. It was scary and deadly silent. The tomb smell the dark past, I guess from the thousands of years old burial. The skeleton had its mouth wide open; looked like it didn't have time to swallow his (he I assume) wealth. The skeleton didn't have much jewelry left on to enjoy in his death or to carry it to the heaven. As I tried to climb up by wedging on the sides, I kept on sliding back down. The six-foot steep tunnel felt like a mile long. I was sweating as I tried to get back. The guide had stayed up at the end of the tunnel. He showed his ugly face at the narrow circular opening, laughing and making remarks in Arabic. After four days in Cairo, it was time to move

Satish D H Thaker

# 9 COFFEE IN ATHENS

Athens, a beautiful clean city with whitewashed houses. On 25 July 1966, we stayed in the side street hotel "Athena". It was challenging to communicate, as not many Greeks spoke English. The Greeks were patriotic. The next morning, we had a continental breakfast in the small chilly room, in the cellar. The breakfast was of a tiny cup of black strong coffee, with a floating layer of coffee powder and a piece of croissant. I missed our traditional mango pickle and the spicy chapatti, with the masala tea to wash it down.

At eight in the morning, it felt like noon already. The hotel was on a quiet street, with a few cars on the road. On the roadside, men queued for boiled eggs for breakfast from a small four-wheeler wooden trolley. The lady selling, shell the eggs, sold them sprinkled with salt and spicy pepper, served on a serviette. It was a traditional Greek-style street breakfast.

The next day we had a trip to The Acropolis of Athens. It's an ancient citadel on a rocky outcrop above the city of Athens. At the highest point sit the great architectural and historic remains of several ancient buildings.

Satish D H Thaker

# 10 GERMANY

From Athens, on 27 July 1966 we flew into Munich. Sankarbhai had been a frequent visitor to Germany for business buying trips for the swimming costumes he sold. He

We travelled by train northwest to Stuttgart. The Germans were particular and punctual with their time keeping, be that with work, train or bus timings. So far on my journey, the quality of cleanliness all around was admirable.

At Stuttgart I parted with Sankarbhai. A disagreement and misunderstanding regarding financial matters flared to mistrust. The arrangement with my dad had been that he would be my chaperone come guardian, right up to England.

Being a strong-headed teenager though, I parted his company in Stuttgart and travelled on my own. He was disappointed but powerless.

On the train to Frankfort, I shared a cabin with two young Spanish brothers and an elderly German gentleman. We conversed in broken English. Two Spanish boys, one German gentleman and an Indian, it was an international gathering. One brother played the guitar, and the other taught me Spanish songs. Frankfurt a 125 miles pleasant train journey to the north. I arrived at the Frankfurt Rail Station late in the evening. The Air India pre-booked flight was from Munich to London, not valid from Frankfurt. My priority was to reschedule the flight from Frankfurt to London. As it was late evening, I spent the night at the station, on a wooden bench. First time in my life, I forced myself to smoke a menthol cigarette to keep warm.

# 11 LANDING IN LONDON

I flew into London on 4 Aug 1966 at the Heathrow, Terminal 3. I was excited but apprehensive to face immigrations. My English was limited to nodding head right and left, up and down, and the words: thank you, yes, no, sorry and ok.

They checked my passport from page to page, and compared the photo with my face. They pointed for me to take a seat. When I was the only one left in immigrations, the officer called me through for further interrogation. He wanted to know who was waiting to receive me.

No one. I didn't know anybody in London.

To Indians, London just meant England.

'Are you going to London?'

'Do you live in London?'

'How long you have been in London?

You could be from Birmingham, Cardiff, and Manchester or from Glasgow, but to Indians, you are from London.

I had a British Colony Passport but not a British Citizen passport. He asked me where I would be staying. I handed over my diary, pointing at dad's friend's address.

He looked at me with raised eyebrows.

My father's friend Mr. Shanghani, whom I had never met, lived nearby the Waterloo Station, in a two-storey four-bed, maybe even five-bedroom house. It was a logging board for newly arrived Indian students, looking for cheap accommodation. Dad had requested that he provide me with accommodation when I arrived so, that's where I would go.

The immigration officers made enquiries about Mr. Shanghani, such as his where-about, to confirm my story. Unfortunately, they couldn't get any confirmation.

They gave me a month-long student visa to get a college admission and then I would have to re-apply for a further extension. He gave me instructions about the taxi stand and how much it would cost to get to the Waterloo Station. He advised me to get the London underground to Waterloo, from Hounslow West, as it was cheaper.

Carrying a large suitcase wasn't a big deal to me. I had an excellent practice carrying a metal trunk, travelling quite often on the train between Bombay and the boarding schools.

From Waterloo Station it was a 15 minutes' walk to Mr. Shanghani's residence.

An English lady was at the door, her eyes were wide open looking a bit surprised. I handed over the diary to her and pointed to Mr. Shanghani's name (I didn't want to make a fool of myself speaking). Still standing on the doorstep, she looked at me again with wide open eyes and tight lips curled in, startled.

She explained, I was at the right address (what a relief), but at the wrong time. It was the school holidays when most families away on long holidays. Mr. Shanghani was away with his family on his holidays. She was a temporary caretaker.

A mobile phone would have been handy (in the 1960's), to ring Mr. Shanghani to   resolve the situation.

Instead, I walked to a nearby hotel. I asked at the reception for a room for a night. Fortunately, the negotiation worked. The male receptionist accepted my Parker Pen as the payment for the room for one night. I wanted to save my cash for rainy days. Being tight fisted-Satish, skipped the meal as it was expensive.

I flicked through my diary, looking desperately for more contacts. Just in-case! I had to find somewhere to go.

Bingo!

Gopalji Patel's address was in my diary.

It was elder brother's handwriting.

He was watching my six.

Jitubhai had mentioned the name a few times in the past.

It was a blessing in disguise.

How strange, though.

Big Bro was in Bombay. Never once had it discussed that I was destined to go to the UK.

He had even put the local bus details to reach Gopalji's address.

House no was 116, in Perry Barr, Birmingham.

The bus going to the Great Barr, on route stopping just before Wellhead Lane. A Red double decker bus no. 35, what a coincidence.

It made me wonder, when did he write the name and address in my diary?

It puzzled me.

I, we, everyone in the Bombay household, knew he was practicing "Numerology".

He told me, my lucky no is 8.

116 Wellhead Lane   and    the bus no 35.

1 + 1 + 6 = 8        3 + 5 = 8

No one had taken him seriously.

God bless him, he made my day.

He put Birmingham in my diary.

That's where I must go.

# 12 BIRMINGHAM

Next day, on 5th Aug 1966, I was on the train from Euston London to Snow Hill Station Birmingham.

Just off the Bull Ring Centre on New Street, as per my brother's note, I caught the no.35 bus. I pointed at the address to the driver, who kindly explained where to get off the bus. Gopalji's road was on the opposite side, 10 yards away from the bus stop on the Great Barr Road.

Carrying a large suitcase (no wheels), I walked 10 minutes to no. 116. *Knock-knock*, I used the heavy brass knockers just above the numbers to announce my arrival.

'Satishbhai? Yes?' index finger pointing at me, with a drop-jaw smile she called me by my name, like she was expecting me.

I had never met her before, but what a welcoming.

She wore a light grey sari and had a center parting raised hairdo, (a popular hair style during the Elvis era). She welcomed me into the house.

She introduced herself as Gopalji's younger sister, Madhu.

Gopalji, big bro's friend, had received a letter to expect me at some stage. Both were staying with their elder niece, Dahiben and brother-in-law Chimanlal.

Gopalji, a lift engineer and Chimanlal worked at the metal foundry and forging manufacturing company. Madhu, waiting for her husband to join her in UK. Both ladies were housewives. Dhaiben had two daughters Gita and Ella, both under 10, and was seven months pregnant.

The two brothers-in-law were at work, expected back home soon, Ladies set the small dining room for a late lunch. My mouth was watering at the smell of traditional Gujarati curry. I couldn't wait. I had missed the home-cooked curry for far too long. The ladies insisted that I should eat without waiting. Who was I, to argue? They served up Gujarati vegetarian Thali with a bowl of chunky potatoes and aubergine mix curry, mango sweet pickle and lime hot-sour pickle, a bowl of daal (soup), and a small side dish of sweet cooked in ghee. The freshly cooked chapattis kept on coming before I had finished even one. That followed with rice and daal. To wash it down, I had a generous glass of jeers butter milk.

Chimanlal, Dhaiben's hubby, the landlord, arrived first. After a brief introduction, we went out for a ride in his car, a Ford Zephyr. The four cylinders, four-door car, manufactured by Ford of Britain from 1950 to 1972.

We picked up Gopalji from his workplace and had a long chat about my journey and his friendship with my elder brother. He was three years older than me. He had come to the UK because of the blood relationship to his elder niece Dahiben.

In the next few days, Gopalji introduced me to his friends Nagin and Ranchhod, all Patels. Our friendship grew. In time they knew us as Four Musketeers.

Chimanlal introduced me to his brothers, cousins and nieces in Birmingham. Most of them were in the Perry Barr area.

It was the summer vacation. The colleges were shut. College admission during the vacation wasn't possible, and the Visa extension, not possible without the College admission. It was a catch 22. I had a dilemma; the temporary visa would expire during the vacation. Thank-fully Gopalji came to the rescue. He assured me that the immigration policies weren't so brutal that they wouldn't understand my situation. He would write to the immigration office and explain my situation.

There were two more weeks to kill. Four of us planned a holiday to North Wales in a Ford Popular two-door car. I volunteered to be the treasurer for the duration of the trip. Everyone chipped in an equal amount and agreed to top it up with equal amounts as and when needed. I took care of the fuel, food and funfair tickets.

The monthly standing order of £10 from dad was sufficient.

Being from the Brahmin family and being a student had a slight advantage, Chimanlal insisted upon no free lodging and boarding.

I received my college admission. Studied Mathematics, Physics, Chemistry, English and Technical Drawing, GCSE "O" Levels at The Brooklyn Technical College near the Great Barr. The daily five-mile walk was to save for the rainy days.

For the first two years, I felt like a headless chicken. I had no direction and no one to guide me. I was the only one of four studying.

Then I met Nirmal Singh Semi. We studied same subjects; in the college and became friends. During my third year in the UK, I lived with the Semi family on Dora Road, just off Coventry Road. On Sundays, we attended prayers at the Ramgadhia Gurudwara and enjoyed lunch together.

**Nirmal and Satish, Brooklyn Technical College**

During weekends we wore same coloured jacket and same style of specs. Funny part was his friends and distant family often mistook me as Nirmal, and called me 'Hi Nimba, kidha hai?', but they caught me out when I tried my Punjabi.

We worked alternate Sundays at Sam's Studio in Balsall Heath, owned by Sam, a Jamaican gentleman. We were only allowed to take family, children, or passport photos. And developed the roll of films. It was challenging to remove the roll of film from the 1" dia. metal casing, dipping in the developer and then in the fixer tank, and then dip in the water container to wash off any chemical, all in the dark room. The wet films were hanged on a string with a wooden pegs to dry.

Sam took care of the local Bangladeshi men, discretely came with a woman from the red-light district, to have photos taken.

Nirmal's dad Gurudial Singh, and an elder brother Chanchal Singh, both were professional carpenters, working on the new residential building constructions site. Nirmal's dad insisted that we joined them during the vacation, rather than sitting idle. For us this meant doing the odd manual non-professional jobs, for cash in hand. Our job was to work as a paddy's mate, riding on a dumper, digging channels to set the road side concrete curbs and some time to get down in the stinking manhole to remove rubbish, with no mask or the gloves For the Jamaican foreman, Nirmal was Singh no1 and I was Singh no 2. Occasionally we took advantage of our similar looks. Mr. Foreman would greet Singh no1 and walk away. Meanwhile Nirmal will move swiftly somewhere else on the far side and start working, the foreman will greet him as Singh no 2. While on that particular day I might be earning cash at the photo studio and also get paid for the manual work I didn't do, Nirmal would clocked his time card and discreetly mine as well.

On night of July 20th 1969, I was with the three generations of Semi family, when the first human landed on the moon. Whole family gather in the large conservatory, seating in the front of the Black & White TV. We witnessed the historic landing, early in the morning.

As the spacecraft came nearer to the moon, the grandparents were adamant and naïve, that they would see the Hindu gods, Lord Rama and Lord Krishna, and goddesses in the paradise. As the understanding was that the paradise is up there.

Post landing, as Neil Armstrong put his foot on the moon, there were no gods.

The grand parents couldn't believe what they witnessed.

'"That can't be the same moon, there are no gods".

They were disappointed and dis-heartened, left the room.

They didn't want to watch the landing, any more.

I saved money doing odd jobs. I finished my GCSC "O" levels at the Brooklyn Tech College and the City and Guild in 'Radio & TV Engineering (evenings classes), at the Mathew Bolton Technical College.

By 1969, Aden was already independent and had become the People's Democratic Republic of Yemen. The Hindus left Aden because it wasn't safe anymore. It was too risky and unpredictable for businesses. My dad preferred India to settle, for his retirement.

It was time to do something different. In 1970 I joined the Royal Air Force.

In 1970s only handful of Indians and Guju's (Gujaraties) were in the RAF (The Royal Air Force).

# 13 HISTORY OF BOMBAY
*Courtesy of:*

*B*ombay, now known as Mumbai, is home to around 10 million people. It is a thriving cosmopolitan, multi-cultural city, and is the centre of India's entertainment industry.

In May 1662, King Charles II of England married Catherine of Braganza, whose family offered a large dowry (a gift made by the father of the bride to the groom). Part of this gift was the Portuguese territory of Bombay. However, Charles II did not want the trouble of ruling these islands and in 1668 persuaded the East India Company to rent them for just 10 pounds of gold a year.

As Bombay was a deep-water port, large vessels were able to dock there. Bombay needed a fort and a garrison of soldiers to protect it from Dutch fleets and Indian pirates.

The city has continued to grow. In 1864, there were 816,562 living there. By 1991, the population of the whole of Bombay (which had spread beyond the islands) was ten millions.

The city changed its name in 1995 to Mumbai, after Mumbadevi, the stone goddess of the deep-sea fishermen who originally lived on the islands before they were driven out by the East India Company

Satish D H Thaker

# 14 HISTORY OF ADEN
## (WIKIPADIA)

## Indian Aden

*B*etween 1839 and 1932 Aden was under the control of the central government in India, specifically Bombay administration.

The Indian diaspora in Aden had great influence in the region because of its economic strength. In fact it has also influenced the culture and social practices in Aden and integrated Indian music, cuisine and costumes into the Yemeni ones.

French social scientist Arthur De Gobineau describes Aden city which he visited in 1855 saying:

'In Aden we saw an Indian city over Arab land amidst rocks.'

In the same context Yemeni researcher Shafiqa Abdullah Al-Arasi says that the Indian influence has become embedded in the Adani society texture.

'During the Indian/British influence in Aden the Indian culture dominated the city as many of the government paperwork was done in English with an Indian style. Even the Arabic songs were played on Indian music and so was the dress-code.'

However, due to politics, the British Empire decided to circumvent the Indian influence and Redirect the governance to London which angered the Indian community in Aden especially the business owners. Great disputes took place between the Indian community and the British government in Aden on this decision and threatened that this will have significant economic consequences.

*Historical documents show that some of the influential Indian businessmen in Aden sent a letter to the British government stating that 'India has more right to Aden than the Brits due to the longer historical and cultural relations India and Yemen.'*

In 1839, Aden became part of the British Empire and was administered by the Bombay Presidency. A garrison of 2000 Indian soldiers was established in Aden and the Indian Rupee was made the official currency. The position of Aden as a gateway to the Red Sea facilitated the visit of several prominent Indian leaders associated with the Freedom Movement to Aden.

Netaji Subhash Chandra Bose made two historic visits to Aden, first in 1919 and later in 1935.

Mahatma Gandhi visited Aden on September 2, 1931, on his way to London to participate in the Second Round Table Conference, accompanied by Pandit Madan Mohan Malaviya, Sarojini Naidu and others, during which he was given a warm reception by the people of Aden.

The Aden administration was separated from India in April 1937 with the appointment of a Governor directly reporting to London. An Indian diplomatic mission at the level of Commissioner was set up in Aden in June 1950.

The Bank of India opened its branch in Aden in 1954 and remained as the only Indian bank in the country until its incorporation by the National Bank of Southern Yemen in 1970, which is now the National Bank of Yemen.

A large number of Indian nationals, including Hindus, Muslims and Parsees, had lived in Aden during mid-1880s until mid-1950s. There is a rich heritage of Hindu, Jain and Parsees temples in Aden and out of ten original temples four survived and one – Mataji Maharaj Temple – is in active use.

## Political Relations in the Modern Times

After India became independent in August 1947, it actively supported the Yemeni struggle for independence from the British Empire. India was one of the first countries to recognise both the Yemen Arab Republic (YAR) after the 26th September 1962 revolution and the People's Democratic Republic of Yemen (PDRY) after its formation on 29th November 1967.

The Indian mission in Sana'a established in 1970 and the relationship started blossoming soon after.

The foreign policies of India and Yemen have much in common. Both are committed to non-alignment, international peace, combating international terrorism, piracy and creation of a zone of peace in the Indian Ocean. Both countries are important members of the Indian Ocean Rim - Association for Regional Cooperation (IORARC), with India assuming the chair from Yemen during a ministerial conference held in Bengaluru in November 2011.

Slowly cinemas spread to the rest of Yemen's southern and eastern provinces, as well as to North Yemen. By the 1950s and 1960s North and South Yemen were home to 49 cinemas. Both men and women used to attend film screenings, and it was a favourite family outing. During this golden era, female artists - such as Sabah Munser, and Fathia Alsagheera - also rose to fame.

Al-Dar al-Ahalih Cinema is the second cinema opened in Sana'a. It opened its doors in 1962 and played primarily Hindi films, which were also the first films to enter Yemen after the formation of the Yemeni Arab Republic.

Hoping to maintain this cultural hub, Hamood's family renovated the building to make it suitable for theatre production. It has since shown a number of popular plays.

Satish D H Thaker

# 15 JAMMAT PARTIES
## (ADEN THIS CENTURY-2000)

*These are wedding celebrations where the Indian community play and sing Indian traditional songs mixed with Yemeni folklore. The women wear "hajala" which is an ankle bracelet and make musical sounds with their steps following Indian dance styles.*

*Khalid Ibrahim Mummin says they have just had one in January this year in Al-Buraiqa and the whole neighbourhood celebrated with them until after midnight.*

*There are several areas in Aden like Al-Qatee', Khassaf, and the Indian district or Hussain district which was called Binian locality in the past.*

*There is also Musafir Khan Area in Crater and which holds a special significance for Indians of older generations because it was the reception and welcoming point for new Indians.*

*In these districts you can find some of the oldest Indian shops such as Rahool's shop for pan and tunbul. Some say this shop goes way back to 1800. The shop sells fofal, Nora, tobacco and special flavours.*

*There is also Abdulnabi's famous shop which dates 1889 and is located in the oldest market in Aden which is Al-Buhra Market, an Indian clan that existed in Aden since the 18th century. They still use terms such as Yihwar which means commercial trading and Abdulnabi's shop is one of twenty similar shops that sell special fragrances, kuhol, incense, body oils and other specially made cosmetics*

*Naser Abdulhussian Abdulnabi Al-Buhri one of the younger generations who opened his own shop says that there is a huge demand for this to the extent that they opened branched in UAE and India.*

*He says many of the Buhra clan had to leave Yemen in the seventies to the gulf countries when conflict took place in Aden because they were peaceful businessmen who did not want their businesses to be affected by the conflict.*

*Abdulmajeed Al-Kashi owner of Abdulkarim Al-Kasho spices shop says it was the Indians who brought dishes such as Zurbian, Biryani, Siadia, Daal and Kajar Halwa. There are other dishes according to Nadira Khan and Farhana such as kulonji, kishra, kari, green sabji, wara potato, shabati bread.*

*The shop sells special spices needed to make these dishes and others although some spices used now in Aden are different from the original ones still used today in India.*

# 16 RAF KHORMAKSAR

## RAF & BRITISH ARMY IN ADEN 1960s
(Source Wikipedia and RAF Khormaksar magazine)

In 60s RAF Khormaksar, Aden was the base for several Squadrons. No 8 Squadron, Sq. badge, A Sheathed Arabian dagger know as a Jambiya, adopted in recognition of the unit's long association with Arabia. Role: Airborne early warning and control.

Moto: Uspiam ET Passim - Everywhere Unbounded.

Formed 1st January 1915 in Brooklands, was disbanded 20th January 1920 at Duxford, but re-formed 18th October 1920 in Egypt.

*In April 1928, No 8 Squadron was posted to Aden.* From 8th March, 1960, the squadron operated with Hunter F, 9 aircrafts in the protectorate policing role. A fighter Reconnaissance policing role was added in 1962, as the Squadrons task.

No. 26 Squadron formed on 8th October 1915. The squadron disbanded in December 1960 at Gutersloh, Germany. *After reformed in 1962, arrived at Khormaksar on 1st March 1963. Remain in Aden until 1965.*

No. 37 Squadron's aircraft at Khormaksar moved from Luqa, Malta in July 1957. One of the oldest Squadron formed on 16th April 1916.

Motto: Wise Without Eyes.

Its four Shackleton long-range Maritime reconnaissance aircraft has flown a total distance of 3,000,000 miles, the equivalent of 120 times around the world. Besides the squadron's search and rescue work, escorting of fighter aircraft in transit, escorting civil and military aircraft in distress, searching for shipping in distress, and dropping life-saving and survival equipment to ditched aircraft.

No. 43 (Fighter) Squadron was formed in April 1916 at Stirling in Scotland. Motto: GLORIA FINIS-Honor above All.
**In early 60s the Squadron was moved to Khormaksar from Nicosia, where it was based for eight months since June 1961.**

No. 78 Squadron was formed as Home Defence unit in 1916. Motto: NEMO NON PARATUS- Nobody Unprepared. Disbanded in 1919 and re-formed in 1936 as Bomber Squadron. Disbanded in 1954 and ***reformed in Aden on 24th April 1956,*** equipped with Single Pioneer aircraft and was reequipped with twin Pioneers in 1958. The Twin Pioneer aircraft, whose short take-off and landing characteristics often make it only plane that can operate into up country air strips, and its main work is short range supply of the Army. Port Squadron, Steamer Point 1964-1966 located in Tawahi shopping district until 1965. Relocated to Ma'alla Wharf, behind the Ma'alla Strip. The task to control movement of civilian and forces personal, baggage, stores and ammunitions.

RAF Hospital, Khormaksar Beach RAFH Khormaksar Beach, a small hospital offshoot of RAF Steamer Point Hospital. Completed 1965 with a helicopter landing pad.

RAF police units served in many locations in Aden. Mainly Steamer Point –Joint services (tri) Provost Units. Various British Army regiments, 3rd Carabiniers-Prince of Wales Dragoon Guards, the Parachute Squadrons, Royal Armoured Corps, Royal Scots Greys, Queens's Own Hussars, The Queen's Royal Irish Hussars QRIH, 4th Royal Tank Regiment, East Anglian 45 Commandos, Paras, served in Aden Protector Area

# 17 HISTORY OF HINDU TEMPLES IN ADEN

*Shree Tricamiraiji-Haveli Temple* Located in Crater's Alasqacani Street, the temple was constructed in 1862.

*Sharee Ramji Temple* Located near the Police Academy College in Tawahi district, it was built in 1875.

*Hanoman Temple* Located in Sheik Othman district, the temple had two lodgings for the Indian community. The temple was built in 1882

*Shree Jain Temple* Located in Crater, it was built in 1882

*Shree Natajee Nandhir Temple* located in Crater and built inside a large cave in the nineteenth century.

*Shree Shankar Hanoman Temple* located in Crater and built inside a large cave in the nineteenth century.

*Shree Century* Located in Holkat Bay, Crater, and the Shree Century had a 99-year lease signed on 29th June 1932.

*Shri Minraj Managi Temple* in Al-Khasaf Street

*Shanker Mindu Temple*, on Queen Arwa road, which was used as a Hindu cemetery for cremation.

Satish D H Thaker

# Parsee Temple

The Zoroastrians (parsees) are a religious order founded by Zarathustra and trace their origins to Iran (Persia). Parsees have always been adventurous and enterprising, and many have travelled to distance shores to seek their fortunes. In as few places they even built an Agiary (Fire Temple) to cater to the religious and spiritual needs of the Parsee community settled on these foreign shores. One such Agairy was built in Crater adjacent to the Playfair Tank, by Parsee Cowasjee Dinshaw Adenwalla. Inside the Adenwalla Agiary the Atash Padsha (Holy Fire) was first consecrated in 1883. The verdant Parsee Gardens within the compound were established over the top of one of the original tanks which from the Tawila Tanks complex.

The Tower of silence, also known as Dakhma, Dokhma or Doogerwadi, is a circular raised structure used by Parsees (Zoroastrians) for exposures of the dead. Zoroastrians consider a dead body to be "nasu", unclean and according to the tradition, the purpose of exposure is to be preclude the pollution of earth or fire. The corpse is placed a top of a tower and so expose to the sun and to birds of prey. In Aden, these birds would have been the kite hawks and crows. Bodies are arranged in three rings, men around the outside, women in the inside circle, and children in the innermost ring. The ritual precinct may only be entered by a special class of pallbearers. Once the bones have been leached by the sun and wind, which can take as long as a year, they are collected in an ossuary pit at the c entre of the tower.

*With the advent of communism after 1967, the Agiary, Dakhma and their funds, etc. all became state property. With all the Parsees set to leave Aden, who would take care of the Atash (the eternal fire)?*

*That's when Cowasjee Dinshaw, the great grandson of Cowasjee Dinshaw Adenwalla who had built the Agiary and Dakhma in Aden in the last century, decided that he would not let the Holy Atash, which had sustained and nurtured the community in this land away from home, just die away. Most of the Parsees in Aden had prospered and done very well for themselves, and they strongly believed it was due to the blessings of the Atash which had provided them with spiritual sustenance and was an important focal point of keeping the Parsee community united, alive and energetic.*

# 18 ARTICLE FROM 'YEMEN TIMES' JUNE 16 2012 ADENI INDIANS: 200 YEARS OF INTEGRATION

*The presence of Indians in Aden dates centuries back to even before the British occupation in 1839. Indian traders and sailors arrived at Aden sea port carrying merchandise and ambitions, and upon experiencing what this coastal town has to offer many decided to settle down and call it a new home.*

*Older generations in the city still recall the image of Aziz, the silent contemplating Indian man who established a bookshop cum library over a century ago, in a Victorian style building at Al-Tawahi district. As you enter this crowded bookshop you are greeted with a smell of Indian incense which he always burned to remind him of home. The place is home to a magnificent collection of Indian, English and some books in other languages depending on the nationalities of tourists or sailors who contributed to the library.*

*It also includes some of the oldest pictures and maps of Aden.*

*However, this valuable treasure has become out of reach since Aziz passed away in 2006 and the younger generation lost interest in preserving it and decided to sell it.*

*The same fate met Barakat Al-Durzei's shop who was the special tailor for the British and Indian soldiers during the British colonization of Aden. His shop was stacked with the long Victorian style military uniforms and even official men's suits with specially decorated cuffs and buttons that were famous in the 19th century.*

*This shop was put out of business when the British left Yemen in 1967. For many years Barakat kept the shop open as a place for people to spend time and read until he finally decided to close it down in 1992 after he distributed all the valuable merchandize to neighbours and friends.*

# A SPECIAL NOTE OF THANKS

54 years ago, in 1966, dad sent me to UK, against all the odds. My uncles were against the idea. I failed the 1st year at Bhavan's College, even still, he planned my journey to London. He kept the plan close to his heart, until the time was right. My mum heavy heartedly said yes, and reluctantly supported dad, so that I could have a better future.

Thank you to all my uncles and aunties, cousins and nieces who helped to dig out the history and the stories about Aden in the 50s & 60s, so I could record it in the book. Also, thanks for the stories about the struggles and the settlement, about friendships and achievements; as well as the stories about tradition and the transition.

To my wife, Kirtida, son Devdutt, daughter-in-law Krishna, daughter Puja (Jaid), who all encouraged me and showed enthusiasm in my writing. My wife has the patience of a mountain. She sacrificed her time and put up with me while I spent hours writing. I had unwritten accountability to the Thaker family.

I'm grateful to Shantibhai and Taruben Patira, Babubhai and Manubhai Vakharia, Kadarbhai and Rangonwala, and Kishore Shrimankar families for supporting me prior to leaving Aden, and after.

Pramila & Anju Mehta (London), Kantibhai (Sankarbhai) and Kantaben Khimji (London), Chimanlal and Dahiben Desai (Birmingham), Gurudayal singh Semi family (Birmingham) and Ramesh Lalbhai Patel (Leicester) for clearing the runway by integrating me in their family. Without their support, I would have struggled to settle and survive.

Mum (late Manorama) and Dad (late Dhirajlal)

I miss you both

# ABOUT THE AUTHOR

Bombay to Birmingham, meant to be author's first book. He started to write and collect informations back in 2014. He spoke and mentioned about it to his friends and family.

But then in 2014, he came across these words, 'The Wake-Up Calls', which diverted his thoughts to write a short book ASAP, before he lose the momentum. The book about the tragic events took place in his life, in a ten years span, while in a partnership retail business. Each event was a Wake Up Call, he kept on ignoring it. And it's about the positive results when he finally woke-up, after the last event, and decided to come out of the business.

'Bombay to Birmingham' is about his journey started from Bombay (Mumbai) in 1966, to Aden (Yemen) to help his dad.

Plan changed in Aden. Author's dad's planned that he would travel with Shankarbhai, as his guardian to Cairo, Athens, to Munich, Stuttgart to Munich, to London.

In Stuttgart plan changed. Having a Powerful Choleric temperament he preferred and decided to travel solo, to London. Instead of settling in London, as earlier, he had to change the plan and travelled to Birmingham.

Hence the Bombay to Birmingham. It is about to be flexible, be prepared to accept the changes and the diversions. Let the universe guide you to your journey, which is most of the time unknown and could be challenging.

He stayed in Birmingham for four years.

In 1970 he joined the Royal Air Force.

Satish D H Thaker

Printed in Great Britain
by Amazon

81032884R00068